HER

A collection of poems about life, love, and second chances

Author: Enzo Morán

JÓVENES ESCRITORES LATINOAMERICANOS
info@mbc-education.com
#JEL **es un grupo de**

MBC-EDUCATION

INDEX

DEDICATION.............................. 9

DESCRIPTION............................. 10

PROLOGUE................................ 11

LOS ANGELES............................ 13

A DRINK................................. 14

WHY DO YOU DRINK....................... 15

ANOTHER NIGHT OUT...................... 16

COP CAR................................. 17

HANGOVER................................ 18

LAS VEGAS............................... 19

AND THE BAND PLAYED ON................. 21

HATE.................................... 22

A BOTTLE OF WINE....................... 23

AN ODE TO NINA SIMONE.................. 24

LOST SOUL............................... 25

THE BRIDGE.................................... 26

INTO THE NIGHT.............................. 28

NO ONE... 29

STRANGER..................................... 30

TONIGHT....................................... 31

THE STREETS AT NIGHT...................... 32

HAPPY.. 33

GUN.. 35

A CONVERSATION WITH GOD................. 36

CONTEMPLATION.............................. 37

THE THING ABOUT LIFE...................... 38

HER... 40

HOW DO YOU.................................. 41

WHAT THEY TELL YOU........................ 42

WHAT I LOVE ABOUT HER.................... 43

HER SMELL..................................... 44

A CONVERSATION WITH FRIENDS............. 46

A CONVERSATION WITH GOD 2............... 47

AT A LOSS FOR WORDS...................... 48

FEAR.............................……...…… 49

WHAT ARE YOU REALLY AFRAID OF?........... 50

OUTBURST.............................….... 51

BOW AND ARROW............................ 52

SHOT THROUGH THE HEART................…... 53

THAT FEELING DEEP DOWN................…... 54

A CONVERSATION WITH FRIENDS 2........….. 55

LET'S HANG OUT............................. 56

CHEAP TRICK.......................…........... 57

TRAVELER...............................…....... 59

YOUR SONG............................…....... 60

IN YOUR ARMS............................…. 61

THE GATES.................................... 62

A Conversation with God 3............... 63

I Wonder.................................... 64

Taking the Road........................... 65

A Conversation with Friends 3........... 66

Spring Chicken............................. 67

A Toast..................................... 68

Wanderer.................................. 69

Lone-Wolf................................. 70

A Promise................................. 72

Could You Still Love Me................. 73

A Conversation with God 4............... 74

In Your Hands............................. 75

Confession................................. 76

To My Parents............................ 78

The Clouds Over Me...................... 80

Your Eyes................................. 81

Kiss the Girl............................... 82

Tomorrow.................................. 84

Broken Glass............................. 85

Lonely...................................... 87

Loving...................................... 88

In The Bedroom......................... 89

One Year Later........................... 90

The Funeral............................... 91

A Simple Man............................. 92

Strike Me Down.......................... 94

The Promise of Tomorrow............... 95

Love.. 96

Goodbye................................... 97

Just Say It................................ 98

As She Looked Into My Soul............. 99

When I Die................................ 100

WHEN SHE CALLED......................... 102

THEM....................................... 104

MICHELLE'S POEM.......................... 106

SARAH'S POEM............................. 107

ALORA'S POEM............................. 108

HER REPRISE............................... 110

AUTHOR AUTOBIOGRAPHY................... 112

DEDICATION

This collection of poetry is dedicated to

Sarah
Michelle
Corey
Blake

Who have been there when they were
needed most, let's try to live a good life

To Alora

For being the light and inspiration when I
needed it most

DESCRIPTION

HER is a collection of poems, some autobiographical, others not so much. It's up to the reader to decide which to believe are true. But all are honest descriptions of feelings from the heart. In Her the reader will find a collection of love poems for the book you're about to read is a love story

PROLOGUE

In this book of poems
You'll find a story
About a man
At the end of the road
Who finds himself lucky
And meets a girl
And meets a new family
And in turn finds the meaning to his life

Enzo Morán

PART I:
SINNERMAN

Where-in the poet describes his life as a lost
soul

Los Angeles

It will be fine
Or it won't
There is no way that it will be fine
And yet we'll still be okay
Me and my friends
We're a disaster
I think that's why we love it here
Because the city is as warm and broken as
we are
Much like the city
You can never actually trust us
We will never get it together
And yet when you're around us
You'll have a blast
Because everyday we wake up
We have to live
So live

A Drink

One drink
Two drinks
Three drinks
Four
Take a shot
Keep drinking
Until tonight becomes tomorrow
Drink to forget
And hope that tomorrow
You don't regret too much
But most important
Tonight
Drink
Drink
Drink
As if your cup is never empty
Drink like tonight is your last tomorrow

Why Do You Drink?

I'm happy when everything's a haze
I forget to be miserable
For when I'm sober
I remember that no one cares
If I live or die
So why do I want to remember that
For when I drink
Everyone's my friend
At the very least the drink is
And the bartender pretends to be
And the wino just asking for a free drink
They may not care if I live or die
But when we drink together
None of us care
We're all just happy
Or at least pretend to be

Another Night Out

Let's go drinking
Let's go smoking
Let's throw a party
Let's do everything we shouldn't
Let's risk our lives
For what's the difference if I live
Until I'm twenty or I'm eighty
For this life is miserable enough
So let's do things we'll regret
Things we hate ourselves for
Let's do them with a friend
So we don't feel so alone
If I'm going to throw my life away
Do it with people I like
So let's get trashy
Let's get stunk
And if we're unlucky
We'll wake up tomorrow
And do it all over again

Enzo Morán

Cop Car

As we walked to the next spot
One of you asked to stop
And you walked to the side
Pulled down your pants
And went on the street
As we all looked out
Someone's eyes sparked open
They mumbled
And stuttered
That's when we saw
The cop car
Coming our way
The pantless one freaked out
When the siren went off
So we made the choice
And ran off
Behind us the sound of the siren wailing
The cop car not far behind
But he didn't care
He just wanted to scare us
A bunch of fools
Just causing trouble

Hangover

Wake up with a headache
Wanting to vomit
Wanting to go back to bed
But I must go to work
Must I go to work?
Do I care about going to work?
I look at the time
7:30 AM
I'll never make it to work on time
So who cares
I'm going back to bed
I have a headache
I don't care if they fire me
I'll never make it to work on time

Las Vegas

I want to write something interesting about
Vegas
But I can't
I remember coming in
I remember leaving
But everything in the city is a blur
Or maybe I'm trying to forget
So far
So good

Enzo Morán

If I stay here
Trouble will find me

Enzo Morán

And The Band Played On

The guitar goes off
Then the band follows
And we lose ourselves to the music
We dance the night away
Not a care in the world
Let's dance the night away
And worry about nothing else
Lost in the crowd
We all just dance
Let's lose ourselves
To the feeling
To the sound
As the band played on

Hate

It stares back at me
The ugly beast
The monster
The thing that has no worth
It disgusts me
Looking at the monster
How could anyone love it
It's the foulest of things
The thing that's so easy to hate
That deserves to be hated
It brings no good
Nothing worth saving
It's the worst of the worst
I can keep going
I can do it for hours
Describing the foul creature
But I can't stand in front of this mirror
forever
I need to step out
So the ugly thing can run around

Enzo Morán

A Bottle of Wine

The one good thing about a drink too far
Is that you'll get the truth
You'll spend your time with someone you
like
Sometimes with someone you hate
And with a drink too far
You'll know their truth
They'll be honest
And so will you
This is where regret comes from
Because you're finally vulnerable
At a time you don't want to be
But in a drink too far
Whether it's a bottle of wine
Or too many beers
You'll be honest
When you're trying to hide

An Ode To Nina Simone

Sinnerman where you gonna run to?
Sinnerman where can you hide?
Sinnerman when will you face the mistakes
of your past
Oh Sinnerman how long can this keep going
You're all alone Sinnerman
And one day it's going to catch up to you
Keep living loose
Keep living "free"
Until the day that the Sinnerman
Is no longer free

Lost Soul

Going out for a drink
It ain't so bad
Especially with friends
Maybe you overdo it
It happens to most of us
But it's not a sin
At worst it's a mistake
The goal is to know when to stop
When to know that you're going too far
A lost soul doesn't know too far
He continues to push
A drink becomes something more
Something life ruining
A point of no return
It's starts with a choice
One thinks it can't be so bad
I will be okay
I'm always okay
Why would this change
So the lost soul
Says yes
To a choice he can't return from
And they find themselves lost
Never to return

The Bridge

Would anyone care
If tonight I disappeared
If I just vanished
Would anyone actually miss me
I don't think so
Nor do I care
For if you don't care what happens to me
I don't have to care about what happens to
you
It makes things easier
I can jump and no one would care
To look down and know
That if I leap no one cares
That's the best kind of freedom
.
.
.
.
I really hope someone cares

Enzo Morán

No Matter What Happens
Don't Lose Your Soul

Into The Night

Look into the night
As it looks back at you
Embrace the night
Walk into it
Do not fear it
For it's always there
Always around
Walk through it
Keep going
Do not fear it
Do not fear the darkness
Let the night hold you
Embrace you
Look into you
Walk with the night
For it can be your friend
But only if you don't fear it
Make the night home
Make it a place
Where you could always be
And you'll never be alone

Enzo Morán

No One

I wanted someone to lie with
I wanted someone to laugh with
I wanted someone to cry with
I wanted someone to share my life with
Most of all I wanted someone to love with
There isn't

Stranger

Everywhere I go I'm a stranger
Stranger here
Stranger there
Stranger everywhere
If only there were a place to go
A place to call home
But I'm a stranger there
So I wander everywhere
For I'm a stranger no matter where I go

Enzo Morán

Tonight

It's nights like these
When we're all together
The messes that we are
All of us trying to find a home
A purpose
A peace of mind
It's nights like these
Where I realize I'm not alone
As I see you all laugh
And share stories
And forget about our troubles
I see that I might have found
Where I belong
Maybe I'm not so alone
For I have all of you
And in these moments
Things aren't so bad
For I found pretend to have found a family
And that's all I could ask

The Streets At Night

Walking the streets late at night
Not sure of where I'm going
I could go to the place I call the house
But it's not a home
Whether I sleep there or on the street
It feels the same
Los Angeles
It's home
So I walk the streets late at night
Looking for an end to the night
Not sure where I'm going
Maybe one day I'll find a home
Tonight will not be the night

Happy

I love to see people happy
Their laughs
Their smiles
Sharing moments with others
Through them I see something I can never
be
I hope to be happy like them one day
I don't know that I'll get the chance
So for the moment
I'll look at others being happy
To help me forget how lonely I am
Keep smiling
Keep Laughing
Keep Loving
I hope to join you someday

Enzo Morán

One Day It Will All Catch Up To Me
But Today Is Not The Day

Gun

There's a gun in my face
I didn't notice at first
The man had just stopped in front of me
And then all of a sudden
There's a gun in my face
And I'm wondering
Is this it?
Is this how I die?
Will it hurt?
I look right at the gun
Waiting for it to go off
I'm going to be shot
This should have just been another night
One where I'm out late at night
And eventually find my way home
But tonight there's a gun in my face
And the man screams
As two others take my things
And I'm still waiting to be shot
As they beat me to the ground
And that's when I realize
In all my self destruction
There are things I want to do
Some things I want to experience
I realize I want to live

Enzo Morán

A Conversation With God

It's been a while since we spoke
I haven't led a good life recently
Sinning more than one person should
Losing myself and hoping to never be found
I've lost my way
But I'm ready to be found
I want to live a good life
I want my people to live a good life
Will you give me a chance
Or have I failed you too often?
I'm going to try to do better
I hope you give me the chance
Cause I really do want to try
To live a good life

Contemplation

I almost died
Would anyone have cared?
With the life I'm living
Should anyone care?
I'm alive for a reason
At least I tell myself that
Then I met her
And maybe there's a reason
She came into my life
Not as someone random
Not as a stranger
But as someone that was always meant to
be there
She came into my life as if she was always
there
I don't know where this will go
I don't know how this will end
But I didn't die
I received a second chance
To live life right

The Thing About Life

We're all born
And then we die
But in between that
So much can happen
We'll suffer
We'll be sad
And we'll have moments of elation
Of pure joy
And we'll never be sure
About what happens next
But in between
There's hope
And in hope
Comes purpose
And comes the try
Because with hope
It makes the sadness easier
That one day we'll be okay
And it makes the joy stronger
In hopes that it lasts forever
The thing about life is
We have to live it

PART II:
Her

Where-in the poet gets a second chance and
falls in love and discovers what it means to
live a
life worth living

Her

I remember everything about the first time
I saw Her
The way her hair was in a bun
Her white sweater
The most beautiful smile I'd ever seen
I even remember the color the day
A pure orange
They say when you fall in love you see
orange
I didn't think of it at the moment
All I knew is that she was special
I remember how when we spoke it felt right
Walking down the street together
I no longer felt alone
I realized in that moment
I deserved to live a good life

How Do You

How do you tell someone you love them
That the moment you see them they
brighten your day
A glance takes your breath away
A smile makes your knees weak
Their laugh gives you life
Their smell gives you a memory of the past
How do you tell them that life with them
Is so much better than without
I guess you just tell them
Don't be afraid

What They Tell You

People say that you must make yourself
happy
You can't let others do it for you
Maybe they're right
But what if you can't
What if you're so lost
And you can't find the way out
Then one day someone comes
And saves you
Through them you become something you
didn't think you could be
Happy
Maybe they're right
Others shouldn't be the reason for ones
happiness
But I'd rather have that
Then continue to be unhappy on my own
So let me be happy
And I'll offer you the same

What I Love About Her

I love the way she looks at the world
That she sees the best in everyone
I love her ambition
How nothing will ever stop her from
reaching her goals
I love her dreams
And how she knows soon they'll be real
I love her smile
The way it lights up every room
I love her laugh
The excitement that it always brings
I love the way she looks at me
And how she takes my breath away
I love how she inspires me
How she makes me into the best version of
myself
But it scares me too
Because of how much I love her
And I'm afraid one day she'll walk away
And I'll only be left with the things I loved
about her

Her Smell

Think of someone you love
And realize that you can smell them
That when you walk somewhere and smell
a similar smell
You think of them
It's instant
And then realize that
You don't know what anyone else smells
like
Because their smell doesn't matter
Not in the way the one you love matters
It's because when you're in love
Your body
Your senses
Are looking for any excuse to think about
them
You know everything about them when
you're in love their
Sound
Look
Feel
Taste
Smell

A Conversation With Friends

She's going to break your heart
Possibly
Maybe
Probably
Hopefully
Because if she does
As much as don't ever want that to happen
It would have meant I was in love
But more important it means I would have
felt loved
So I hope my heart isn't broken
But if it is, it would have been worth it
So I'll take the leap
Love her as I can
And if my heart breaks
I won't have an ounce of regret

Enzo Morán

Why Should Any Of Us
Wait To Live Our Lives

A Conversation with God 2

This feels like a trick
To bring her into my life
To introduce someone who fits well
That makes sense
I'm apprehensive because it feels like a trap
It this my JOB moment
Where you introduce the thing I need
And then take it away?
I hope not
Because for the first time I'm happy
Don't take that away

At A Loss for Words

I wish I had a proper way to describe it
And the truth is there may not be
But if you're lucky in life
You will sometimes become close to
someone
Who looks at you with such care, adoration
and love
That it will undress and overwhelm you
And if you're someone who has been hurt
You'll try to run away or hurt them
So that they can never see you be
vulnerable
But realize that that someone is a gift
I remember the first time she looked at me
that way
And I wanted to tell her in that moment
That I loved the way she looked at me
Because it felt as she saw me as someone
Better than I was
To feel so much compassion, care and
fascination
I wish for everyone to have that moment

Fear

If you'd search my soul all you'd find is
Doubt
Fear
Anxiety
A feeling of worthlessness
Any excuse to keep me from trying
And then I met you
The things you saw in me
Ambition
Happiness
Love
You saw something worth saving
Where I saw something that was lost
You saw something with purpose
And one day I woke up and saw what you
saw
A soul worth saving
I was looking for someone to lie with
I was looking for someone to cry with
I was looking for someone to laugh with
But more importantly
I was looking for someone to love
And love me back
And maybe I found it

What Are You Really Afraid Of?

Once upon a time
There was a boy
And he was all alone
And he met a girl
Who was also alone
But together they had each other
So they fell in love
Or so he thought
They'd spend countless hours together
Even more talking on the phone
They didn't like being apart
Together they were whole
And then one day
The girl walked away
She no longer needed him
To fill her lonely heart
So in an instant she threw him away
And that's when he found out
She never loved him
She just needed a body to use
So he never wanted to fall in love again
For why would next time be any different
So he chose to live a lonely life
Until now

Outburst

In wasting so much time
In waiting to tell her how I feel
To waste time
On something so simple
I should just tell her the truth
Who cares about the fear
It only leads to living in regret
Instead I'm here having this feeling of
Wanting to say something
And not having the balls to say it
I need to stop being a coward
Stop
Being
A
Fucking
Coward
The worst that can happen is she doesn't
Feel the same
And guess what you're back where you
Started
But if you wait
And never say anything
You'll never know
And instead she'll fall in love with another
And you'll live in regret

Bow and Arrow

I guess it's time
To take a risk
If I want to be loved
I have to give my heart away
It's possible they'll drop it
And it will shatter
But it's much better
Than to keep feeling this way
I don't need a reason
To love you
To give you my heart
I just hope you don't drop it
And it breaks
I just want to be your man
And for you to be my woman
A thousand flowers will bloom
If we fall in love
So please take my heart
And I'll be your man
And you'll be my woman

Shot Through The Heart

Maybe I'm a fool
That every time I think of you
It feels like a shot through my heart
It was a scary feeling at first
I wasn't sure what to make of it
The feeling made me fall to my knees
Wanting to say words I was too afraid to
say
Hoping that you'd be the one to say them
first
When you're around I feel fine, I feel good
Even if the shot through my heart
Still scares me a little
I now know what it likes to feel alive

Enzo Morán

That Feeling Deep Down

It's fine to feel lonely
It can be frightening
The feeling of being alone
For it means
You think that no one is there for you
But in your loneliness
Remember this
It also means you're alive
And if you're alive
There's a chance for a better life

A Conversation with Friends 2

Tell her you love her
But what do I say?
Tell her you love her
But I'm afraid
Just tell her you love her
But what if she doesn't love me back?
Dear god man, just tell her you love her
And what if she laughs?
Then she laughs
And you're sad
And we'll be sad together
But at least you'll know
And if you're lucky she'll love you back
So tell her you love her
We hope for the best
We want to see you happy
So even if the answer is not what you want
You'll know
And who knows maybe she'll love you back
But dear god man, tell her you love her
Or at least ask her out

Let's Hang Out

Let's go to a movie
Let me buy you a snack
Let's have a good time
Let's just hang out
And have a good time
Let's see if we make sense
Or at the very least lets have one day of fun
So let's go to a movie
Do you want to see a concert?
Or what is it that you would like to do?
As long as it's with you
In can be anything in this world

Cheap Trick

It's been a long day
Longer than either of us would have liked
But the journey had to be made
And now we're headed home
We're both so very tired
As you drive us down the coast
I turn on the radio
And old song finishes playing
And the next one starts
I remember it perfectly
It's Cheap Trick's
I want you to want me live at Budokan
And as the song plays
I look at the ocean
And then I see the way the sun lights your
face
And in that moment I see
How perfect life can be
No matter what happens tomorrow
We'll always have today

Enzo Morán

Tell The Girl That You Love That You Love Her

Enzo Morán

Traveler

I was once a lonely traveler
Going down a path I didn't know
I wasn't sure what I was looking for
Just walking down an empty road
Telling myself one day I'll be okay
But I didn't know what to do
I just walked a path hoping for the best
Something that would lead me to
something good
But every path I took
Just stole a piece of who I am
Every path I took was the wrong one
Or maybe there was no good path for
someone like me
Yet I was still a traveler looking for the
right path
And a piece of me constantly ripped apart
Until there was almost nothing left
And then I took my final path
The one that was supposed to break me
And at the end
There you were
And for once in my life
I had taken the right path
Because it saved the last piece of me

Your Song

I wrote you a song
It goes like this
F major
G minor
A minor
A minor
G minor
D minor
F major
G minor
D minor
G minor
C major
F major7
I'd love to play it for you someday
I think it's quite lovely
There are lyrics too
I'd write them down
But there only for you
Let me sing it to you someday
I think you'd like it

Enzo Morán

In Your Arms

When I'm in your arms
It is as though I'm finally home
In a place where I've always belonged
I no longer feel like running
From hiding
When I'm in your arms
And you are in mine
It is as though nothing
In this world
Can stop me
For I have found a place
That makes me invincible

The Gates

The earth
The stars
The heavens
None of them can keep me from you
I will meet the devil
And stand at his gates
And walk over him if he were
To attempt to keep me from you
I would walk through heaven
And face God himself
And if he were to stand in front of me
And keep me from you
Then I'd look at him
And remember that he created me in his
image
And therefore I am him. And he is me
And we are one in the same
and that my love for you
In this moment
Makes me stronger than him
So I'd walk through him
And ask for forgiveness
And he'd accept my forgiveness
For we are created in his image
And my love for you was a gift from him

A Conversation With God 3

There are moments where I've lost my faith
When I've cursed you
When I wanted to stop believing
I've taken too many hits
Life just constantly punches me in the face
And yet when I've been angry at you
I can't stop believing
And the reason might be selfish
But it's kept me believing
So even when I've been angry
I've kept believing for a simple reason
If you are up there
And heaven too
When I go
I'll get to see the ones I've lost
At least once more
And recently I've met the best people
And if I were to lose them
I get to see them once more
So even when I've almost lost faith
I don't stop believing
On the chance that I'll see them all again

Enzo Morán

I Wonder

I wonder if she knows
As she reads through this book
That she's the reason
It exists
And if she does
Will we ever speak of it?
Or will it be unspoken

Taking the road

Spending my days
With the woman I love
Looking at her when she's asleep
I realize that life
May not give me many perfect moments
But I should be grateful for the moments
I have with her
I'd take her hand
And I'd follow her to the end of the world
Listen to what I say
Take your chances
For you'll never regret it
You might just walk the world
With the person you love
The person you need
And no matter what hardships you hit
Together you'll overcome
Take any road together
And you'll both be okay

A Conversation with Friends 3

We just want you to be happy
I know I responded
They didn't know
Nor did I in the moment
With those simple words
The last bit of me
That hid from the world
Had been broken
For a long time
I tried to hide away
To trust no one
For sooner or later they would all leave me
But with those words
I made the mistake of opening my heart
And for not one moment did I regret it
With these people
With her
I was happy
I was at peace
I looked forward to tomorrow

Spring Chicken

The feeling of jumping out of bed
Of wanting to start the day
Of looking forward of what's to come
Never would I have thought that would be
me
But there you were
With sweet love
And care
A look from you
That makes me melt
And jump out of bed
To start my day
And do what I have to do
So that at night I can come back to you

A Toast

Let's have a toast
To my friends
For you've seen my at my worst
And now you're here to see me at my best
Who have always been there
Let's have a drink
But just one
Because we only have one life
To live
To dream
To do everything we've always wanted

Wanderer

Whether you know it or not
As you walk through this world
You leave a mark
The goal is to leave one that make people
remember you fondly
You may not think that your presence
matters in the smallest moment
But by simply being there
You've made an impact
Now the goal is to make it a good one
To have the people that will remember you
Remember you fondly
That when they think of you
They smile
They miss you
They hope you lived a life worth living

Lone-Wolf

I've never needed anyone
Never will
I've always figured it out
Besides you all leave anyway
So we meet for a moment
And we have a good time
But the party always ends
So don't get attached
Because I sure don't
Because sooner or later
Everyone leaves
This is why I don't get close
Because even when they say it won't ever
end
We know it's not the truth
So I don't worry when they're finally gone
.

.

.

And the I met all of you
My defenses fell
For the first time I felt something new
I felt complete
This time I didn't want to run
I wanted to try

I didn't push anyone away
Instead I embraced it
Will I regret it?
I don't know
Nor do I care
Truth is no matter what happens
I probably won't
Because I finally feel whole

A Promise

It's hard to admit
To come to terms
That I have been the problem
And not the world
That I have pushed everyone away
They are habits I'm attempting to stop
To hopefully outgrow
Please be patient
Sometimes I still make mistakes
And sometimes it feels like I'm pushing you
away
But please know I'm not trying to hurt you
It's hard to do better
To change
But I'm trying
Please be patient
I promise it'll be worth it

Could You Still Love Me

If you knew my truth
If you knew of the things that I've done
Could you still love me
For all my faults
And the mistakes I've made
If I were to tell you my story
With warts and all
The times I've been hurt
And the times I've hurt
The long days
And the even longer nights
Would you still love me
Knowing that I've done wrong
Is me attempting to be better enough
Or did I sin for too long
Would you believe me
If I said I've changed
Could you still love me
For the mess that I am

A Conversation with God 4

Was this always the plan?
For me to get so lost
For a moment
So that when something good finally
happened
I'd appreciate it
Was this your plan?
For me to be a fool
For me to hurt
And make mistakes
So I can appreciate when the good came
There must have been a better way to have
done this
But I won't question it
I'll just send my thanks

Enzo Morán

In Your Hands

There is nothing more
Powerful
Terrifying
Significant
Than holding someone's love in your hands
And even if you don't love them back
Be gentle to their love
Even when letting them down
For it's the thing
You'd want someone to do for you

Confession

I've never said this outloud
I don't know that I ever will
It's still hard to talk about
And I know you'll all look at me strange
But I wanted to die
I wanted it to just end
For it to be no more
I wasn't okay
Not in the head
And I didn't know what else to do
I didn't want to burden anyone
Besides they probably didn't care
So I decided to die
And it would be fast
And easy
And only a little painful
But it would have saved me the time of a
miserable life
Never have I been happier to give
something a second chance
Life threw me something
I didn't know I needed
But it was a gift
For not taking a final step
It's hard

Life that is
And sometimes you come close
To saying goodbye
It's just the thing that makes the most sense
But if you do
You'll miss out of the perfect moments
Like when you finally find yourself in a
room with people who care about you
When you're driving down the road to the
perfect song
When you're home alone and want to cry
And then you get that call, or that text
Or when she looks at you
And doesn't say a word
And you think
Wow
I can't believe I'm alive

To My Parents

You made mistakes
As did I
I won't mention them
For you never really liked to talk about
them
Things were never easy
Even when you tried
The mistakes that were made
Are forgiven
There is love
There was also hate
There was anger
Some still lingers
There's no need to ask for forgiveness from
either side
The choices that were made are ones we
must live by
If you're burdened by them
Forgive yourself
For it's the only way to move forward
To my parents
Things were never easy
And things may never be okay
But they never need to be
I think we've all tried to move on

To build a bridge upon the ashes
We seem to be doing well
All of us now
Or as well as one can
There were many lessons
What to do
And what no to
To be a parent isn't an easy life
Mistakes will always be made
All we can do is grow together
To do better each day
For tomorrow could be our best day
Just know that we're doing well now
Better than before
Now more than ever let me free
As you're set free
Live a happy life
Bask in the light

The Clouds Over Me

Just another cloudy day
No sun in sight
I'd like to see the light
It looks like it'll rain
I haven't seen the sun in days
Hoping for the clouds to lift
Hoping the light comes in
I look at the clock
The sun should be out
But outside is just another overcast day
So I lay on the couch
Waiting for the sun to come out
Maybe if I close my eyes
Then the sun will come out
So I close my eyes
And as I open them after a few moments
I see you looking at me
Wondering why I'm just laying there with
my eyes closed
And I see you look at me
I see the sun take a peek
And it's a wonderful sunny day

Your Eyes

You can't break my heart in hurting me
In rejecting me
In shouting at me
Tell me I'm useless
Or ugly
Or anything that you think can hurt me
The only way for you to break my heart
Is to see you cry
For it means I have failed you
And that's a feeling I can do without

Kiss the Girl

I'm afraid to get up
I don't want to fall
I'm afraid to do anything
I don't want to fail
Everything is going so well
But what if today is the day when it goes
wrong
Today I'm really afraid
I see you come into frame
Today I'm afraid
To talk to you
To smile at you
To be in your presence
Today's the day where it could all change
Today I'm afraid to come looking for you
I'm afraid of how you look at me
And then I stop and take a breath
And I tell myself
Don't be a fool
Go kiss the girl
And so I walk to her
She gives me a funny look
I hesitate
Don't be a fool
So I kiss her

Enzo Morán

And she kisses me back

Enzo Morán

Tomorrow

If I sleep
And don't wake up
And my last memory
Is of you
Then I couldn't ask
For anything better

Enzo Morán

Broken Glass

I'm not asking you to heal me
To be my bandage
I simply hope that you see
A broken man
Become whole
And to know
Because of you
He will once again
Be complete

Enzo Morán

To Love Someone Is A Beautiful Feeling
Only Outdone By The Feeling Of Being Loved

Lonely

I like the feeling of loneliness
For when I'm alone
I long for you
I wait for you
And when I see you
I love you more

Loving

You do me a favor
In letting me love you
For it reminds me
What it's like to be alive
To let go of the selfishness
To know one can feel this way
In letting me love you
I'm reminded why I look forward to waking
up
To be a better version of myself
To find meaning in the small things
To breathe in
And out
The favor you do me
Is giving me a second chance

In the Bedroom

Let's call out
Let's never get out of bed
We don't have to go work today
We have everything right here
So why don't you call out
And get back to bed
One day won't be the end of the world
So get back in bed
For we're all we need
One day won't end the world
So let's call out
And get back to bed
Enjoy right now
So let's call out
And get back to bed

One Year Later

A year ago
I was a mess
Now I'm not the same man
I use to be
I'm so much better
I'm doing things I never thought I could
Who would have thought
All I needed was someone to smile back
To change my life
To find my meaning
To take a leap
I still don't understand what I did to
deserve this
Or maybe it's an opportunity
To live the life of a good man
Where I don't go off and hurt myself
But instead I live this life
With you
With them
With those who care
I got a second chance
And so far I haven't blown it

Enzo Morán

The Funeral

He died
He finally died
After years of living a life of sin
Of debauchery
Doing the kinds of things
That would catch up to one eventually
They finally did
And he died
And at his funeral
No one mourned
No one cared
He was all alone
As he was supposed to be
He wouldn't missed
He shouldn't be missed
In fact
When he died
There was a party
A celebration
He was finally dead
The demon had finally gone to his grave

Enzo Morán

A Simple Man

I don't need to be rich
I don't need it all
Not a big house
Or a fancy car
I'm happy with a simple life
A simple home
A simple car
As long as I'm with you
I'm the richest man there is
Because with you in my life
I couldn't ask for anything more

Enzo Morán

If you're afraid to love
Then you're afraid to live

Strike Me Down

If I'm to die in this moment
So be it
For now that I look back
I've lived a good life
And though I want more time
To tell more stories
If I'm to die in this moment
I've lived a good life

The Promise of Tomorrow

There is no guarantee
Nothing is promised
No fixed order
Nothing is predetermined in this world
Tomorrow like today
Will always be different
Your life isn't set in stone
Everyday is a chance for you to do
something new
Because tomorrow is not promised
To live in fear
Is to not live for tomorrow
To live in regret
Is to live your life in the past
So live the life you want today
That can lead in an unpromised tomorrow
Love in spite of fear
For tomorrow could be better

Love

Love is the only thing where you willingly
subject yourself to pain
Even in it's best moments
Love will hurt you
The same way it can bring out the best in
you
It can also bring out the worst
But it's only because it's one of the few
things that's inevitable
Whether we like it or not
At one point we'll all fall in love
And at one point it'll be the best feeling in
the world
At another the worst
But even at its worst
We can all agree
We won't ever regret it

Enzo Morán

Goodbye

If you are to leave my life
Please say goodbye
It's all I ask
It's not a demand
But a favor
For having you leave
Will hurt enough
But if you just say goodbye
At least I get to see your eyes one last time
And that's all I'll need
So if you are to step out that door
At the very least
Say goodbye

Just Say It

I want to tell you how I love you
But I'm afraid
Not that you won't feel the same way
But that I'll lose the way you look at me

As She Looked Into My Soul

As you read this book
Whether you ever do
Know that no one
Knows me like you do
You've made me vulnerable
And I've trusted you
And told you my life
My secrets
Even these pages don't know the story
But you
You know it all
My hurt
My happy
My heart
Because only you have been able to see into
my soul
To see who I am
To see my worth
And so I told you my story
And you listened
And she told me yours
So I knew you were the one to tell my story

When I Die

My biggest fear
For when I die
Was would anyone come to my funeral
Or would I be another forgotten soul
I may have pretended to not care
But I never wanted to end alone
And now I know
That when I die
Someone will be there
But not only that
More than one
For those who love you
Will be there
Both in life and when you're gone
It's nice to be loved

Enzo Morán

I don't need to be remembered as a great man
Just one who was loved

When She Called

The joy
The optimism
The feeling that everything will be okay
Life had given a gift
Everyday was worth waking up for
To have people who mattered
To have someone to love
To finally love oneself
And that's when she called
The woman who had scarred me
Who made me feel like like I never could
love again
The one who took someone so broken and
built him up
Just to break him again
She called
To ask how I was doing
And every feeling I once had came rushing
back
A part of me wanted her back
My lips quivered
As she continued to speak
To ask how I was doing
And I thought of the answer
Long and hard

How was I doing?
I thought of it for a moment
Was I really happy
And I smiled
Because I thought of my friends
The people who loved me
Who cared about me
And I thought about her
Who made me realize that I could love
And I told the woman on the phone about it
all
And on the other side she was silent
She told me she was happy for me
I wished her luck
And the call ended
Never to hear from her again
I was no longer broken
And I hope she wasn't either
But hers was not my life to live
And mine was not hers
Now my life was for me
And them

Them

Our first night together
I don't remember
We went out
We laughed
I hope we didn't cry
But we all had a good time
We all felt at home
I didn't realize in that moment
What I had found
I'm pretty sure we've all felt the same
In this moment
And many after
We had found home
Family
Those who would be there for us
We'd be there for each other
You've seen me at my worst
And I the same
We've shared pain
Heartbreak
Joy
Regret
And I continue to look forward to it all
For I have found what I've been seeking
A family to call my own

Five misfits
Trying to figure it out
I don't know that we ever will
Maybe we shouldn't care
For through it all
The good, the bad
We'll have each other
And that's all I could ask for

Michelle's Poem

Do you remember how we met?
With mutual friends
It was nice
We talked
But I'm sure neither of us thought we'd be
close
And then time flew by
And we became friends
Someone who I could confide in
When I was sad
When I needed someone to talk to
When I needed someone to talk me out of
doing certain things
Even though I never listened
But again you never listened to my advice
either
Two messy friends
Hoping for each other's best
Hoping for each other to figure it out
To my friend
Who puts up with my nonsense
To my friend
Who picks up the phone

Enzo Morán

Sarah's Poem

In you I found a kindred Spirit
Someone who pushed the limit
Or maybe we just don't know any better
We're both risk takers
Maybe a little too risky
A bit messy
Sometimes a lot of messy
Always pushing the other forward
A bit of a bad influence on each other
Who calls me out
No one has ever been as mean to me as you
You know what I'm talking about
And yet they were words I really did need
to hear
And you have to admit, you care
It's nice to have another person who cares
Even if they're a little mean

Alora's Poem

She woke up
Like she did everyday
With a sense of optimism
With passion in her heart
With the goal to turn her dreams into
reality
Each time she got out of bed
She did it with intent
To make the world a better place
To be kind
To be the light
To inspire those around her
And even though some days weren't easy
Sometimes life wasn't kind
And things felt difficult
Nothing could ever defeat her
For she knew
The only thing
That could stop her
Was herself
And therefore she was unstoppable
So she walked with a purpose
To be the change
The brightness
The kindness we all need

Enzo Morán

She hoped that she inspired
And whether she knew it or not
Everyday she did inspire
She made others want to be better
To the see the good in themselves
To try a little harder
She is strong
She is hope
She is Alora

Her Reprise

To live in darkness
Is so much easier
To hide from the world
To not let them know how you feel
The darkness is home
It's safe
Why open yourself up to the possibility of
pain
Through the lack of optimism
You live a clearer life
Don't let the sun in
Never let the sun in
Ignore it
Turn your back to it
One day I let the sun in
She came unexpectedly
It caught me off guard
I was never to let the sun in
And it came in
With a force
And I didn't know what to do
So I let her in
And I realize
What a fool I've been
To live in darkness

Is to be a fool
To be constantly shrouded in fear
The darkness is not a friend
But the thing that holds you back
Through the sunshine
You find life
Meaning
Purpose
Let it in if you haven't
I'm not saying you won't be hurt
I'm saying for whatever happens
If you let the sunshine
It's light
It's warmth
It will be worth it
In the sunshine you'll find life
It will show you to live
So live

BIOGRAFÍA DEL
AUTOR ENZO MORAN

Enzo Moran is a writer from Los Angeles, California raised by immigrant parents fleeing a civil war. A passion for storytelling came swiftly and from a young age he knew that he wanted to tell stories whether it were a film, poetry, a play and everything in between, and now he belongs to the Latin American Young Writers organization and is a self proclaimed Bohemian much to the chagrin of those close to him. Enzo Moran has attempted to make a career through his art while working in different fields such as the veterinary medical field. His goal is to be able to use his art to inspire many and to one day create a system that can be used to support artists of every background.